Apes and Monkeys

KINGFISHER

Published in 2011 by Kingfisher
an imprint of Macmillan Children's Books
a division of Macmillan Publishers Limited
20 New Wharf Road, London N1 9RR
Basingstoke and Oxford
Associated companies throughout the world
www.panmacmillan.com

ISBN 978-0-7534-3160-3

First published as *Kingfisher Young Knowledge: Apes and Monkeys* in 2004
Additional material produced for Macmillan Children's Books by Discovery Books Ltd

1 3 5 7 9 8 6 4 2
1TR/0511/WKT/UG/140MA

A CIP catalogue record for this book is available from the British Library.

Printed in China

Note to readers: the website addresses listed in this book are correct at the time of going to print.
However, due to the ever-changing nature of the internet, website addresses and content can
change. Websites can contain links that are unsuitable for children. The publisher cannot be held
responsible for changes in website addresses or content, or for information obtained through
a third party. We strongly advise that internet searches be supervised by an adult.

Acknowledgements
The publisher would like to thank the following for permission to reproduce their material. Every care has been taken
to trace copyright holders. However, if there have been unintentional omissions or failure to trace copyright holders,
we apologise and will, if informed, endeavour to make corrections in any future edition.
b = bottom, *c* = centre, *l* = left, *t* = top, *r* = right

Photographs: *cover* Shutterstock Images; 4–5 Steve Bloom; 6–7 Oxford Scientific Films; 8 Martin
Harvey/NHPA; 9 Ardea; 10–11 Ardea; 11*tl* Oxford Scientific Films; 12*br* Oxford Scientific Films; 13*tl* Oxford
Scientific Films; 14 Ardea; 15*t* Rojer Eritja/Alamy; 15*b* Steve Bloom; 16 Oxford Scientific Films; 17 Steve
Bloom; 18*b* Anup Shah/Nature Picture Library; 20*tr* Oxford Scientific Film; 22*b* Steve Bloom; 23*tr* Peter
Blackwell/Nature Picture Library; 23*l* Art Wolfe/Getty Images; 23*br* James Warwick/NHPA; 24*bl* Ardea;
24–25 Steve Bloom; 25*br* Ardea; 26*bl* Kevin Schafer/Corbis; 26*t* Tony Hamblin/Corbis; 29 Mark
Bowler/NHPA; 30–31*b* Richard du Toit/NHPA; 31*tl* Anup Shah/Nature Picture Library; 31 Roland Seitre/Still
Pictures; 32*bl* Oxford Scientific Films; 32*br* Ardea; 33*tl* Oxford Scientific Films; 33*r* Anup Shah/Nature
Picture Library; 34*bl* Theo Allofs/Corbis; 34*r* Ardea; 35 Steve Bloom; 36*b* Anup Shah/Nature Picture
Library; 36*t* Getty Images; 37*tl* Dietmar Nill/Nature Picture Library; 37*b* Frank Lane Picture Agency; 38*b*
Anup Shah/Nature Picture Library; 38*t* Ardea; 39 Getty Images; 40*tl* Ardea; 40*b* Karl Ammann/Nature
Picture Library; 41 Ardea; 48*t* Shutterstock Images/Cloudia Newland; 48*b* Shutterstock Images/Stéphane
Bidouze; 49*l* Shutterstock Images/Jackiso; 49*r* Shutterstock Images/Anan Kaewkhammul;
52*l* Shutterstock Images/Bernhard Richter; 52*r* Shutterstock Images/Stacey Bates; 53 Shutterstock
Images/namatae; 56 Shutterstock Images/Mertens Photography

Commissioned photography on pages 42–47 by Andy Crawford.
Thank you to models Aaron Hibbert, Lewis Manu, Alastair Roper and Rebecca Roper

discover science

Apes and Monkeys

Barbara Taylor

KINGFISHER

Contents

What is an ape?

You are one! There are four other great apes – gorillas, chimpanzees (chimps), orang-utans and bonobos. Gibbons are small apes. Apes have gripping fingers and thumbs and no tail.

Hairy apes

Apes are a kind of mammal, which is an animal with a hairy body. Hair helps to keep mammals warm. We have much less hair than the other apes, such as this gorilla.

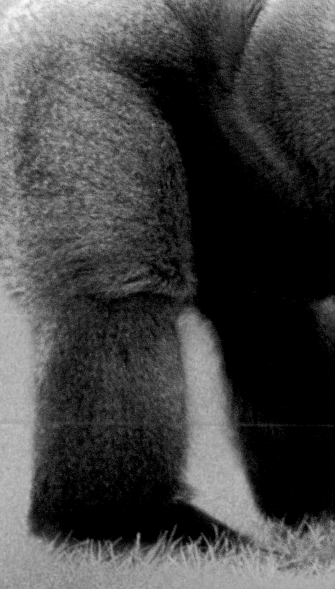

Brainy apes

All apes have a big brain and are clever. They can solve problems, use tools, remember things and communicate with each other. Humans are the only apes that speak.

Arms and legs

Most apes' arms are longer than their legs. They can swing through the trees or walk on all fours. Humans walk upright on long legs.

Apes in Africa

Three big wild apes live in the forests, woodlands and mountains of Africa. These are gorillas, bonobos and chimps. They all live in large groups.

Gorilla groups

Gorillas live in peaceful groups with between five and 20 members. The group of males, females and young is led by a big male.

bonobo

chimpanzee

Girl power

Bonobos look like chimps but are more graceful. They have smaller heads and ears and longer legs than chimps. Female bonobos lead the groups.

Noisy chimpanzees

Chimps live in the biggest groups, with up to 100 members. A few important male chimps lead each group. Chimps are noisier and fight more often than the other African apes.

Apes in Asia

Orang-utans and gibbons are apes that live in Asia. They spend a lot of time in trees, although male orang-utans have to climb down sometimes, as they grow too big for the branches.

Fatty faces

Male orang-utans have fatty pads the size of dinner plates on their faces. These make them look bigger and help them to scare away any rivals.

Singing apes

Siamang gibbons are the biggest gibbons. They sing to tell other gibbons where they live. Pouches on their throats inflate as they sing, making their voices even louder.

Getting around

Chimpanzees and gorillas spend a lot of time on the ground. Orang-utans, gibbons and bonobos climb in the trees. Gibbons live high in the tree-tops.

Knuckle walking

When they walk on all fours, chimps rest their weight on thick pads of skin on their knuckles.

Swinging ape

Gibbons swing from branch to branch using first one hand, then the other. They can move very quickly without making much noise.

Hanging on

Orang-utans grip branches tightly with their long, hooked fingers. Their arms can stretch a long way. Each arm is nearly twice as long as each leg!

Finding food

Apes feed mainly on fruit and leaves but they also eat a small amount of meat, such as insects. Chimps sometimes eat larger animals, including monkeys.

Going fishing!

Chimps chew sticks or grass stems to make them the right shape to dig for food. They push the sticks into a termite mound. When they pull them out, termites are clinging to the end.

Fruit feast

Durian is one of the orang-utan's favourite foods. They remember where to find trees with ripe fruit.

Tasty termites

Millions of termites live
inside a termite mound.
They can provide a tasty
snack for hungry
chimpanzees.

Brainy apes

Apes are one of the few animals
to make and use tools, which
is one sign of an intelligent animal.

Tough nuts to crack

Some chimps bang a heavy
stone on to nuts. This works
like a hammer and cracks
open their hard shells.

Rainy days

Apes do not like
the rain because
their fur is not
very waterproof.
This orang-utan
has made its
own umbrella
out of bark.

Chatty chimps

The chimpanzees in a group make different sounds, pull faces and use the position of their bodies to 'talk' to their family and friends.

Pulling faces

With their big eyes and bendy lips, chimps are good at pulling faces. Their expressions show how they are feeling.

Playtime

As young chimps play, they learn how to mix with other chimps in their group. They learn which chimps are the most important in the group.

Sound signals

Chimps use their big ears
to listen for sounds drifting
through the forest. The
members of a group
hoot to each other to
stay in touch.

Forever friends

Chimps may have special
friends in their group.
These friends hug each
other for comfort and
to show that they
are still friends.

Baby apes

Apes usually have one baby at a time. They spend many years teaching the baby how to move, feed and behave.

Gibbon families

Gibbons live in small family groups. A gibbon father plays with his baby and helps to look after it.

Riding piggy-back

Many baby apes, such as this gorilla, are carried around until they are strong enough to walk by themselves.

Motherly love
A baby orang-utan lives with its mother for seven to nine years. It does not usually have any other playmates.

What is a monkey?

A monkey is a clever, playful mammal with a tail. It usually lives in groups for safety. There are 130 different monkeys, from tiny tamarins to big baboons.

Living quarters

Monkeys live in a wide range of habitats, from forests and mountains, to grasslands and swamps. These proboscis monkeys live in a swamp.

Terrific tails

Monkey tails can be long
or short, thick or thin,
straight or curly.
This colobus uses
its fluffy tail to
steer as it leaps
through the trees.

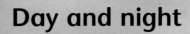

Day and night

The owl monkey
is the only
monkey that
comes out at
night. It has big
eyes to help it
see in the dark.

How clever?

Capuchins are
intelligent
monkeys with
a large brain.
This helps them
to live in a range
of different habitats.

American monkeys

American monkeys live in the warm rainforests of Central and South America. They have wide, round, far-apart nostrils. Many have prehensile tails, which are tails that grip like an extra hand.

Finger food

Tamarins have long fingers, which they use to search for their insect food. They have claws instead of fingernails.

Tree-top leapers

Little squirrel monkeys
leap through the trees
like squirrels, and climb
on to thin branches.
They live in big groups
of up to 200 monkeys.

Furry monkeys

Saki monkeys have long
shaggy fur, which helps to
protect them from heavy
rain. They may suck water
off their fur.

African and Asian monkeys

These monkeys have nostrils that are close together, and hard pads on their bottoms to help them sleep sitting up. They do not have prehensile tails.

Packed lunch

The red-tailed monkey stores its food in cheek pouches, then finds a safe place to sit and eat.

Follow the leader

Slim, graceful mona monkeys live in troops of up to 20 monkeys. Each troop is led by a strong male. Monas have striking marks and colours on their soft, thick fur.

Hot baths

Japanese macaques live in the mountains. In the cold, snowy winter, they grow thick coats and sit in hot spring water to keep warm.

Spot the difference?

Monkeys are smaller than apes and not as clever. Monkeys usually have a tail, but apes never have a tail.

Big ape

Gorillas are the biggest of the wild apes. Female gorillas weigh about half as much as males. The size of the males scares predators and rivals.

Monkey tails

The spider monkey curls its prehensile tail around branches. The bare, ridged skin under the tail helps it to cling tightly.

Moving and grooving

Monkeys scamper along the tops of branches or run fast along the ground. They do not usually swing through the branches, like the apes.

Feet made for walking

Baboons live on the ground and walk on all fours. They press their fingers on the ground, but keep their palms raised. This lifts their heads, so they can watch for danger. They even walk through water.

Leggy leapers

The long back legs of colobus monkeys help them to push off strongly from branches. They can make huge leaps from tree to tree.

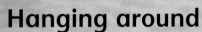

Hanging around

Uakaris live at the tops of tall trees in swampy and flooded forests. They sometimes use their powerful back legs to hang upside-down.

Hungry monkeys

A monkey's favourite food is usually fruit. Monkeys also feed on leaves, nuts, flowers and insects. Some have special diets, such as the marmosets that eat tree gum.

Nuts and seeds

Sakis spend a lot of time eating seeds. Some sakis have strong jaws to crack open hard nuts and reach the soft food stored inside.

Clever capuchin

This capuchin is chewing bark from a small branch. It can also crack open nuts or shells by hitting them on rocks.

Meat for dinner

Baboons are strong, smart and agile enough to catch other monkeys, birds and small antelope.

Green salad

Colobus monkeys mainly eat leaves, but also enjoy munching ripe fruit, flowers and seeds. In their big stomachs, bacteria release energy from their food.

Getting to know you

Monkeys have many ways of keeping in touch. They also use calls, colours and behaviour to find a mate and warn of danger.

Keep away!

Howlers are the world's noisiest land animals! Their calls warn other howlers to keep away.

Bad hair day?

Monkeys and apes groom each other's fur. They pick out any dirt or bugs they find and clean up any scratches. Grooming helps monkeys keep clean and stay friends.

Colour signals

The colours of the male
mandrill become brighter
when he is healthy, angry
or excited. Females prefer
males with bright colours.

Baby monkeys

Monkey mothers look after their babies until they are about 12 to 18 months old – a shorter time than apes.

New babies
Baby monkeys have their eyes open at birth and can cling to their mother's fur.

Baby-sitting
Langur mothers let other females hold and look after their babies. This makes their lives easier.

Mother's milk

Like other mammals, vervet monkey mothers make milk in their bodies to feed to their babies. They have to eat a lot of food to give them enough energy to make this milk.

Watch with mother

Monkey babies, like this spider monkey, cling to their mothers. They watch the other monkeys in the troop to learn how to climb and leap, which food is good to eat, and how to behave.

Apes and monkeys in danger

All the apes (except humans) and many monkeys are in danger of becoming extinct. The main problem is humans.

Ape crisis

Some of the apes, including the white-handed gibbon seen here, could be extinct in just 20 years. We must do more to protect them from hunting and habitat destruction.

Disappearing act

Marmosets, like this tufted-ear marmoset, have lost their forest homes. They are also caught and sold as pets.

Monkey madness

The rare Chinese golden monkey is threatened by hunting for its meat and fur. The trees in its forest home are also being cut down.

Saving apes and monkeys

We can help to save apes and monkeys by protecting their habitat, breeding rare ones in zoos, and finding ways for people and wild animals to live together.

Special survivor

Golden lion tamarins have been saved by protecting their forest homes in Brazil.

Finding out more

We need to find out more about apes and monkeys so we can help them survive. Scientists, like Dr Jane Goodall (right), study chimps and work to save them and their habitats.

Orphan apes

If a mother ape dies or is killed, her baby needs a lot of love and care. People sometimes look after these orphans, and may one day release them back into the wild.

Monkey mobile

Make a monkey chain

Follow steps 1 to 5 to make one monkey. Then make more monkeys and hook their arms together in a long chain.

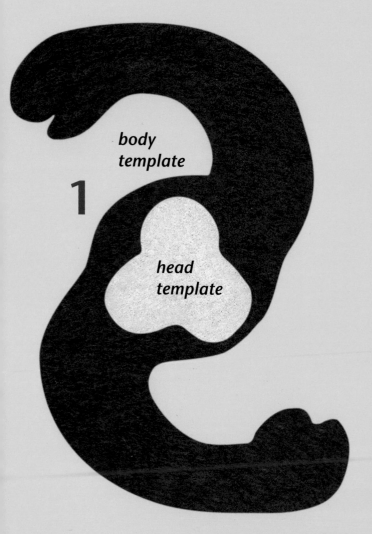

1

body template

head template

Trace the two templates in pencil and transfer the outline shapes on to a paper plate.

2

Using the scissors, carefully cut out the card templates. Hold the edge of the plate with one hand to stop it moving.

3

Fold a piece of brown felt in half and secure it with a pin. Trace around the body template with marker pen, then cut out.

You will need

- Tracing paper
- Pencil and black marker pen
- Paper plates
- Scissors
- Brown and cream felt
- Safety pin
- Glue

Glue the felt body shapes to the back and front of the card shapes. Make the faces from cream felt and glue them on.

Cut out four small 'D' shapes and glue them on as ears. Use a black marker pen to draw on the eyes, nose and mouth.

Termite towers

Eat like a chimpanzee

Make your own termite tower. Then put food inside and use a straw to get the food out. It is not as easy as it looks!

You will need

- Cardboard tubes
- Sticky tape
- Scissors
- Paper plate
- Pencil
- Newspaper
- Glue or flour
- Water
- Kitchen paper
- Poster paints
- Paintbrush
- Sweets
- Drinking straws

Find four clean cardboard tubes and tape them together with sticky tape. Ask a parent or friend to hold the tubes still.

Turn a paper plate upside-down. Hold the four tubes over the plate and draw around them with a pencil.

Using the scissors, carefully cut out the holes in the paper plate. Then tape the tubes firmly in place over the holes.

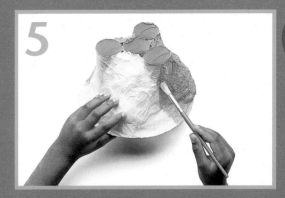

Screw up pieces of newspaper and stick them into the gaps between the tubes. This should make a mound shape.

Mix flour and water together or use glue to paste strips of kitchen paper and newspaper over the mound. Paint it to look like mud.

Choose some sweets that are larger than the end of a straw and place them in the tubes. Suck through a straw to pull up the sweets. How many can you catch?

Monkey masks

Make a monkey face

Monkeys and apes have round heads
which are perfect for making masks.
Find your favourite monkey or ape
in the book and make a mask of its face.

You will need
- Felt tip pen
- Tracing paper
- Coloured felt
- Scissors
- Glue
- Paper plate
- Elastic

1

Draw the head of the monkey
on to tracing paper. Place this on
to brown felt and carefully cut
out around the outside edges.

2

Trace the face shape of the
monkey on to tracing paper.
Put this over the cream felt
and cut it out.

Glue the cream felt on top of the brown felt and stick them both on to a paper plate. Glue white rings around the eyes.

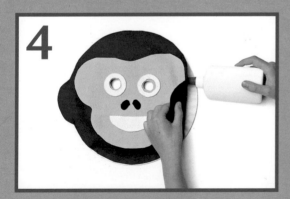

Glue on a felt nose and mouth. Then cut out eye holes and tie or glue elastic to the sides of the mask to hold it on.

Glossary

Bacteria – tiny one-celled lifeforms

Bonobo – a species of ape, similar to a chimpanzee but smaller

Communicate – to make other animals understand your message

Diet – the food an animal usually eats

DNA – stands for deoxyribonucleic acid, the material that our genes are made of

Durian – a large, very smelly fruit

Expression – the 'look' on a face

Extinct – when an animal species has completely died out

Forest – a very large area of trees

Groom – to pick through fur with fingers

Habitat – an area where an animal lives

Inflate – to fill up with air

Intelligent – clever and able to understand things easily

IQ – stands for intelligence quotient, a measure of a person or animal's intelligence

Knuckle – one of the joints where a finger bends

Mammal – an animal that feeds its babies on mother's milk

Orphan – having no mother or father

Predator – an animal that hunts and eats other animals

Prehensile tail – a tail that grips tightly

Rival – a competitor for food or mates

Tool – an object that helps with work

Troop – a group of monkeys

This book includes material that would be particularly useful in helping to teach children aged 7–11. It covers many elements of the English and Science curricula, especially animals and habitats, and some cross-curricular lessons involving Maths, Geography, PE and Art.

Extension activities

Writing
Each double-page information spread has a title, introduction, and three or four paragraphs of text, each with its own sub-heading. Use this structure to write a report about orang-utans, using the information on pages 10, 12, 13, 16 and 21. Now do the same for a report about humans.

Using the information on page 28, draw a table to show the differences and similarities between apes and monkeys.

Find all the ways that apes and monkeys use tools (see pages 14–15, 16, 32). Either write a report on it, or make up a story about monkeys where tools are an important part of the plot.

Speaking and listening
Read about the dangers to apes and monkeys on pages 38–39 and 40–41. Prepare a one-minute presentation about how we can help them survive.

Science
Apes are mammals. What are the other five groups of animals? (Answer: birds, reptiles, amphibians, fish, invertebrates).

Find information about monkey and ape diets. Draw a food web to show who eats what. Research their predators and add them to the web. (Diet information is on pages 14, 32–33).

Page 22 lists the different habitats monkeys live in. How are these habitats different? Present your information as a report or table. How do monkeys survive in them?

Cross-curricular links

Geography: Find all the countries and continents mentioned in the book, sometimes hidden in the names of animals. Use an atlas to find where they are in the world. Which is nearest to you? (Answers: Africa pages 8–9, Asia page 10, Central and South America page 24, Japan page 27, China page 39, Brazil page 40).

Geography/Writing/Art: Three different types of gorillas live in Africa: western lowland, eastern lowland, and mountain gorillas. Draw a map of Africa including a key to show where each type of gorilla is found. Describe the terrain using words and/or pictures. (This links with the topic of ecosystems and biomes.)

Maths: Read page 12. Draw some orang-utans of different heights, making sure their arms are twice as long as their legs.

Research to find the heights and weights of several different apes and monkeys. Make two graphs, one to compare heights and the other to compare weights.

PE: Copy the different ways apes and monkeys move (see pages 12–13, 30–31).

Using the projects

Children can follow or adapt these projects at home. Here are some ideas for extending them:

Page 42: Make your mobile look like a different type of monkey or ape.

Page 44: Change the game so that you have to use chopsticks (like the apes that use sticks on page 14).

Page 46: Read the information about expressions on pages 18–19. Can you make masks with different designs and colours to show different feelings?

- It is easy to tell the difference between apes and monkeys: monkeys have tails, apes do not.

- Monkeys use their voice, facial expressions and body movement to communicate.

- The smallest monkey in the world is the pygmy marmoset. It measures 117–159 millimetres and weighs between 85 and 140 grams (about as much as a mobile phone!).

- The howler monkey is the loudest monkey: its howls can be heard from about 3 kilometres away.

- In zoos young gorillas receive the same injections as human babies, because gorillas can pick up the same diseases as humans.

- Orang-utans make a new nest in the trees every night to sleep in.

- Orang-utans can live for up to 50 years in the wild.

- Gorillas are the largest living primates. They can grow to over 2 metres tall, and weigh up to 230 kilograms – about the same as three men!

- When a monkey yawns it usually means it is either tired or angry.

- Bonobos sometimes use sticks to defend themselves.

- Chimpanzees communicate in similar ways to humans: by hugging, kissing, holding hands and tickling.

- Monkeys groom each other to show affection.

- Orang-utans are some of the most intelligent primates and are able to use a variety of tools.

- Chimpanzees are the closest relative to humans: they share 98 per cent of our DNA.

Apes and monkeys quiz

The answers to these questions can all be found by looking back through the book. See how many you get right. You can check your answers on page 56.

1) Why do male orang-utans have fatty plates on either side of their face?
   A – To make them look bigger and scare away any rivals
   B – To hear better
   C – To attract a mate

2) Which is the biggest gibbon?
   A – Lar gibbon
   B – Silvery gibbon
   C – Siamang gibbon

3) How many different types of monkey are there?
   A – 13
   B – 130
   C – 1,300

4) Which of these monkeys only comes out at night?
   A – Proboscis monkey
   B – Colobus monkey
   C – Owl monkey

5) What do colobus monkeys usually eat?
   A – Leaves
   B – Eggs
   C – Worms

6) What do marmosets eat?
   A – Tree gum
   B – Insects
   C – Fruit

7) How long does a baby orang-utan live with its mother for?
   A – Between seven and nine weeks
   B – Between seven and nine months
   C – Between seven and nine years

8) What does the colobus monkey use its tail for?
   A – To steer as it leaps between trees
   B – To protect itself
   C – To clean itself

9) Why do saki monkeys have long shaggy fur?
   A – To protect them from hot sun
   B – To protect them from heavy rain
   C – To keep them warm

10) Where do Japanese macaques live?
   A – In the desert
   B – By the sea
   C – In the mountains

11) What part of their hands do chimps use when they walk on all fours?
   A – Palms
   B – Knuckles
   C – Fingertips

12) Which is the only ape that can speak?
   A – Gorilla
   B – Human
   C – Orang-utan

Find out more 55

Books to read
Animals, A Children's Encyclopedia (Visual Encyclopedia), Dorling Kindersley, 2008

Baboon by Louise Spilsbury, Raintree, 2011

Everything You Need to Know About Animals by Nicola Davies, Kingfisher, 2010

Gorillas (Animal Lives) by Sally Morgan, QED Publishing, 2005

Monkeys and Apes (100 Facts) by Camilla de la Bedoyere, Miles Kelly Publishing Ltd, 2010

Orang-utans (Animal Lives) by Sally Morgan, QED Publishing, 2007

Places to visit
Edinburgh Zoo
www.edinburghzoo.org.uk
Edinburgh Zoo has a huge number of animals to observe. Notably it has a specialized chimpanzee enclosure called the Budongo Trail where visitors can look at the chimps close-up.

Monkey World Ape Rescue Centre
www.monkeyworld.org
Monkey World in Dorset helps governments around the world prevent the illegal smuggling of primates. It is home to numerous refugee monkeys including orang-utans, gibbons, chimpanzees and squirrel monkeys.

Bristol Zoo
www.bristolzoo.org.uk
Bristol Zoo has a specialized gorilla enclosure where visitors can observe a family of six gorillas. There is also a monkey jungle with a large variety of monkeys on display.

Websites
National Geographic
www.nationalgeographic.co.uk
The National Geographic website has lots of information on monkeys, apes and gorillas.

BBC Animals
www.bbc.co.uk/nature/animals
On this website you can find out all about your favourite animals, the habitats they live in, what they eat and how they survive. There are also video clips of each animal from BBC documentaries.

Apes and monkeys quiz answers

1) A	7) C
2) C	8) A
3) B	9) B
4) C	10) C
5) A	11) B
6) A	12) B